THE PLUMROSE
HEALTHIER EATING COOKBOOK

WENDY SWEETSER

MARTIN BOOKS

OVER 70 TASTY RECIPES
ALL PHOTOGRAPHED IN FULL COLOUR

Published by Martin Books
Simon & Schuster Consumer Group
Fitzwilliam House
32 Trumpington Street
Cambridge CB2 1QY

in association with
Plumrose Ltd
PO Box 25
Willerby
Hull
HU10 6DR

First published 1991
© Simon & Schuster 1991

ISBN 0 85941 668 2

Design & typesetting: Ken Vail Graphic Design, Cambridge
Photography: Peter Chambers
Food preparation for photography: Andrea Wright
Printed and bound in Great Britain by:
    HarperCollinsManufacturing, Glasgow

Cover recipes (front to back): Sweet and Sour Chicken and Frankfurters (page 38); Salami, Red Pepper and Mozzarella Salad (page 15); Pork and Vegetable Samosas (page 64).

Notes on recipes
Ingredients are given in both metric and imperial measures; use either set of quantities, but not a mixture of both, in any one recipe. All spoon measures are level standard measuring spoons unless otherwise stated.

Wendy Sweetser is Cookery Editor of *Woman's Realm* magazine and has contributed articles to a wide variety of other leading publications; she has appeared on television and worked with many major food companies in developing and promoting new products. *The Plumrose Healthier Eating Cookbook* is her fourth cookery book.

CONTENTS

FOREWORD

Welcome to the Plumrose Healthier Eating Cookbook!

This cookbook shows how versatile and convenient Plumrose products really are. We hope that you will enjoy trying the brand-new recipes and that, in time, they will become firm family favourites.

Whether you need to prepare a hearty meal for all the family, tasty packed lunches or something special for the children, you will find a recipe here to fit almost any occasion.

The variety of uses for Plumrose products is almost infinite, from salads and sandwiches to main meals, picnics and snacks.

Whilst Plumrose is still best known for their ever-popular cans of Chopped Ham with Pork, the Plumrose range has grown significantly in recent years, as you can see below.

4

FOREWORD

Now there are safe modern plastic tubs of Farmhouse Spreading Pâté in nine tasty flavours. Three new ranges of foil-packed meats, presented in eye-catching cartons – twelve delicious varieties in all. You can store all these products in the pantry or cupboard, because just like cans they keep fresh without refrigeration.

Then there is the brand-new range of Plumrose Chilled Meats in clear packs. Over twenty different meats in all shapes and sizes for your convenience. Pre-sliced square for sandwiches, and round or oval for salads, or Plumrose Joints which can be sliced thick or thin for greater versatility – all Plumrose Chilled Meat larger packs are now re-sealable.

Cooking with Plumrose is delicious and easy, with each pack showing why eating with Plumrose is 'healthier eating'.

So please go ahead and enjoy the Plumrose difference.

FILO PURSES

Serves 6

FILLING:
2 tablespoons sunflower oil
4 spring onions, sliced
1 celery stick, chopped finely
50 g (2 oz) mushrooms, chopped finely
50 g (½ pack) of Plumrose Bavarian Style
Ham Sausage, chopped
85 g (3 oz) Brie, chopped
salt and freshly ground black pepper

PASTRY:
4 sheets of filo pastry
3 tablespoons sunflower oil

1 Preheat the oven to Gas Mark 4/180°C/350°F.
2 Heat the oil and sauté the onions and celery until soft but not brown. Add the mushrooms and cook for one minute. Remove from the heat, transfer to a bowl and allow to cool.
3 Mix in the ham sausage, Brie, and seasoning.
4 Brush the sheets of filo pastry with oil and layer on top of each other. Cut into six 12.5 cm (5 inch) squares.
5 Divide the filling between the squares and gather up the pastry to enclose the filling. Pinch together at the top to seal.
6 Place on a greased baking sheet and brush with oil. Bake in the oven for 15–20 minutes until golden and crisp. Serve hot.

TUNA-STUFFED TOMATOES

Serves 6

6 large tomatoes
185 g can of Plumrose Tuna Chunks in Brine, drained
and flaked
1 tablespoon snipped fresh chives
1 small celery stick, diced finely
85 g (3 oz) Brie, cut into small dice
6 tablespoons low-calorie prawn cocktail sauce
salt and ground white pepper

TO GARNISH:
seedless green grapes

1 Cut the flower end off each tomato (the opposite end to the stalk). Reserve the tomato tops. With a small serrated or grapefruit knife cut out the centre pulp and pips, taking care not to break the skin.
2 Stand the tomatoes upside-down on a plate and leave to drain for 15 minutes.
3 Meanwhile, in a bowl, mix together the tuna, chives, celery and Brie. Stir in the prawn cocktail sauce and the seasoning.
4 Spoon the tuna mixture into the tomato shells and replace the tops at an angle. Stand on serving plates and cover with clingfilm until needed. Serve each tomato garnished with a tiny bunch of seedless green grapes alongside.

Filo Purses,
Tuna-Stuffed Tomatoes,
Cauliflower and Ham Chowder (page 8),
Ham and Pea Soup (page 8)

CAULIFLOWER AND HAM CHOWDER

Serves 6

2 tablespoons sunflower oil
2 celery sticks, chopped
1 cauliflower
225 g (7½ oz) potatoes
600 ml (1 pint) chicken stock
600 ml (1 pint) semi-skimmed milk
170 g can of Plumrose Chopped Ham with Pork
326 g (11 oz) can of sweetcorn kernels
170 g (6 oz) Cheddar cheese, grated
salt and freshly ground black pepper

TO GARNISH:
chopped fresh thyme

1 Heat the oil in a large saucepan and fry the celery for 3–4 minutes until it starts to soften.
2 Cut the cauliflower into small florets. Cut the potatoes into small chunks. Add to the pan with the stock and milk, and bring to the boil. Cover the pan and allow to simmer for about 15 minutes until the cauliflower and potatoes are tender.
3 Cut the chopped ham with pork into 1 cm (½ inch) slices and add to the pan with the sweetcorn, cheese and seasoning.
4 Stir over a slow heat until the cheese melts but do not allow to boil. Serve hot, sprinkled with chopped fresh thyme.

Pictured on page 7

HAM AND PEA SOUP

Serves 6

2 tablespoons sunflower oil
1 onion, chopped
1 carrot, chopped
225 g (7½ oz) dried peas, soaked overnight
1.1 litres (2 pints) chicken or vegetable stock
255 g carton of Plumrose Lean-n-Tasty Ham, diced finely
salt and freshly ground black pepper

Freezing: possible

1 Heat the oil in a large saucepan and fry the onion and carrot until soft but not brown.
2 Drain the peas and stir into the pan with the stock. Bring to the boil, cover and simmer for 2 hours or until the peas are tender.
3 Cool slightly, then purée the soup in small quantities in a food processor or liquidiser.
4 Return to the rinsed-out pan and stir in the ham. Add the seasoning and bring back to the boil over a gentle heat. Serve with toasted bread croûtons.

Pictured on page 7

HAM AND COTTAGE CHEESE MOUSSE

Serves 6

100 ml (4 fl oz) unsweetened apple juice
2 teaspoons gelatine
200 g pack of Plumrose Sliced Ham, minced
100 g (4 oz) cottage cheese, sieved
4 tablespoons low-calorie mayonnaise
1 teaspoon French mustard
salt and freshly ground black pepper

TO GARNISH:
cucumber slices

1 Pour the apple juice into a small bowl and sprinkle the gelatine over it. Stand the bowl over a pan of simmering water until the gelatine is dissolved.
2 Meanwhile, in a bowl mix together the ham, cottage cheese, mayonnaise and mustard.
3 Fold the gelatine into the ham mixture and add the seasoning.
4 Spoon into a glass serving bowl, level the top and leave in a cool place until set.
5 Garnish with cucumber slices. Serve with wholemeal toast.

Pictured on page 11

HAM AND CHICORY TARTLETS

Serves 6

PASTRY:
100 g (4 oz) wholemeal flour
100 g (4 oz) plain flour, sifted
100 g (4 oz) block margarine, diced
2 teaspoons chopped fresh thyme
a little cold water

FILLING:
1 tablespoon olive or sunflower oil
1 button onion or shallot, chopped finely
1 head of chicory, sliced
56 g (½ pack, 2 slices) of Plumrose Apple Ham, chopped
200 ml (7 fl oz) semi-skimmed milk
2 (size 3) eggs, beaten
salt and freshly ground black pepper
2 tablespoons grated Parmesan cheese

Freezing: possible

1 Preheat the oven to Gas Mark 5/190°C/375°F.
2 To make the pastry, place the flours in a bowl and rub in the margarine. Mix in the thyme and enough cold water to make a soft dough.
3 Knead on a slightly floured surface until smooth then roll out to line 12 tartlet tins.
4 To make the filling, heat the oil and sauté the onion or shallot until soft but not brown. Add the chicory and cook for 3 minutes.
5 Remove from the heat and stir in the ham. Allow to cool.
6 Spoon the mixture into the pastry cases. Beat together the milk, eggs and seasoning and pour carefully over the top. Sprinkle with the cheese. Bake in the oven for 15 minutes until the filling is set. Serve hot with a small salad garnish.

Pictured on page 11

SEAFOOD LETTUCE CUPS

Serves 4

4 large iceberg lettuce leaves
2.5 cm (1 inch) piece of cucumber, diced finely
1 small orange, divided into segments
185 g can of Plumrose Tuna Chunks in Brine,
drained and flaked
100 g (4 oz) peeled prawns
150 ml (¼ pint) low-calorie mayonnaise
1 teaspoon lemon juice
4 tablespoons low-sugar tomato ketchup
2 gherkins, chopped very finely
salt and paprika
a little grated orange rind

1 Wash and dry the lettuce leaves and arrange on four serving plates or in small bowls.
2 In a bowl mix together the cucumber, orange segments, tuna and prawns and divide evenly between the lettuce cups.
3 Mix together the mayonnaise, lemon juice, tomato ketchup and chopped gherkins until smooth. Add the seasoning.
4 Spoon the sauce over the tuna mixture and sprinkle with a little grated orange rind. Serve with thin rounds of wholemeal French bread, lightly toasted.

Ham and Cottage Cheese Mousse (page 9),
Ham and Chicory Tartlets (page 9),
Seafood Lettuce Cups

TURKEY AND CUCUMBER PUFFS

Serves 8

CHOUX PUFFS:
50 g (2 oz) block margarine
150 ml (¼ pint) water
100 g (4 oz) wholemeal bread flour
4 (size 3) eggs, beaten
salt and freshly ground black pepper
2 tablespoons chopped mixed nuts

FILLING:
200 g pack of Plumrose Turkey Slice, chopped
5 cm (2 inch) piece of cucumber, diced finely
3 tablespoons soured cream
1 tablespoon creamed horseradish

TO GARNISH:
cherry tomatoes
watercress sprigs

Freezing: possible (unfilled choux puffs)

1 Preheat the oven to Gas Mark 7/220°C/425°F.
2 To make the choux puffs, cut the margarine into small pieces and heat with the water in a saucepan until the margarine has melted.
3 Bring to a rolling boil, then remove from the heat and add all the flour. Beat with a wooden spoon until the mixture forms a soft ball and leaves the sides of the pan clean.
4 Beat in the eggs a little at a time, then add the seasoning.
5 Spoon into a large piping bag fitted with a 1 cm (½ inch) plain nozzle and pipe 8 éclair shapes on to a dampened baking sheet. Sprinkle with the chopped nuts.
6 Bake in the oven for about 30 minutes until firm and well browned. Remove from the oven and cut a slit in the side of each choux puff. Return to the oven for 5 minutes.
7 To make the filling, mix together the chopped turkey slice, cucumber, soured cream and horseradish.
8 When the choux puffs are cooked split each one in half and spoon a little of the filling into the centre. Serve while still hot, garnished with cherry tomatoes and watercress sprigs.

*Turkey and Cucumber Puffs,
Pineapple with Ham, Chicken and Peanuts (page 14),
Pasta Broth (page 14)*

PINEAPPLE WITH HAM, CHICKEN AND PEANUTS

Serves 4

1 tablespoon sunflower oil
1/2 green pepper, de-seeded and chopped finely
50 g (2 oz) dry roasted peanuts, chopped
255 g carton of Plumrose Savoury Roll, Ham and Chicken Variety, chopped
4 slices of fresh or canned pineapple
1 tablespoon chopped fresh coriander

TO GARNISH:
fresh pineapple or herb leaves (optional)

1 Heat the oil and sauté the pepper until soft but not browned.
2 Stir in the peanuts and ham and chicken roll and cook for 2 minutes to heat through.
3 Place the pineapple slices on serving plates and spoon the ham and chicken mixture into the centre of each slice. Sprinkle with the fresh coriander. Decorate the serving plates with fresh pineapple or herb leaves, if liked. Serve at once.

Pictured on page 13

PASTA BROTH

Serves 4

2 tablespoons sunflower oil
1 leek, sliced
300 g can of Plumrose Pork Luncheon Meat, chopped
397 g (13 oz) can of chopped tomatoes
600 ml (1 pint) chicken stock
100 g (4 oz) pasta bows
1 teaspoon dried marjoram
salt and freshly ground black pepper
100 g (4 oz) frozen peas

Freezing: possible

1 Heat the oil in a large saucepan and cook the leek over a gentle heat until soft but not brown.
2 Add the luncheon meat, tomatoes and stock. Bring to the boil.
3 Add the pasta, marjoram and seasoning. Cover the pan and simmer for 10 minutes.
4 Stir in the peas and bring back to the boil. Simmer for a further 5 minutes or until the pasta is tender. Serve hot with crusty wholemeal bread.

Pictured on page 13

SALAMI, RED PEPPER AND MOZZARELLA SALAD

Serves 4

2 red peppers
225 g (7½ oz) mozzarella cheese, sliced or
cut into sticks
100 g pack of Plumrose Danish Salami
a few coriander leaves or sprigs of frisée lettuce

DRESSING:
1 garlic clove, crushed
2 tablespoons sherry vinegar
2 tablespoons olive oil
1 tablespoon chopped fresh coriander
1 teaspoon lemon juice
salt and freshly ground black pepper

1 Grill the peppers until the skins turn brown and blister. Cover with a damp cloth until cool enough to handle, then peel away the skins.
2 Cut the peppers in half, discard the seeds, and cut into small pieces. Slice the cheese or cut into sticks.
3 Arrange the peppers, cheese and salami slices on a serving plate. Decorate with coriander leaves or sprigs of frisée lettuce. Cover with clingfilm until ready to serve.
4 To make the dressing, whisk all the ingredients together or shake well in a screw-top jar. Spoon over the salad just before serving.

Pictured on page 17 and the cover

SPINACH AND TUNA ROULADE

Serves 4–6

FILLING:
198 g can of Plumrose Tuna Steaks in Oil, drained
1 hard-boiled egg, chopped
4 tablespoons low-calorie mayonnaise
1 teaspoon lemon juice

ROULADE:
300 g (10 oz) packet of frozen chopped spinach, thawed
4 (size 3) eggs, separated
1 tablespoon snipped fresh chives
salt, freshly ground black pepper and a pinch of nutmeg
25 g (1 oz) grated Parmesan cheese

1 Preheat the oven to Gas Mark 5/190°C/375°F.
2 Grease a 33 × 23 cm (13 × 9 inch) swiss roll tin and line with non-stick baking parchment.
3 To make the filling, place the tuna in a bowl and break up with a fork. Stir in the hard-boiled egg, mayonnaise and lemon juice until combined. Set aside.
4 To make the roulade, dry off the spinach in a pan over a gentle heat until excess moisture has evaporated.
5 Transfer the spinach to a bowl and stir in the egg yolks, chives and seasoning.
6 Whisk the egg whites until stiff and fold into the spinach mixture. Pour into the lined tin and bake in the oven for 12–15 minutes until set and springy to the touch.
7 Allow to cool for 5 minutes then place a sheet of greaseproof paper on the work surface and sprinkle with the Parmesan cheese.
8 Turn out the roulade on to the greaseproof paper and peel away the lining paper.
9 Spread the filling over the roulade to come within 1 cm (½ inch) of the edge. Roll up from one long side, using the greaseproof paper to help. Serve hot or cold, cut into slices. To re-heat: preheat the oven to Gas Mark 4/ 180°C/ 350°F. Place the roulade on a baking sheet and heat in the oven for 15 minutes.

Pictured on page 17

TUNA PIPERADE

Serves 4

2 tablespoons sunflower oil
1 red pepper, de-seeded and chopped
56 g (½ pack, 2 slices) of Plumrose Smokey Ham, chopped
2 × 185 g cans of Plumrose Tuna Chunks in Brine, drained
8 (size 3) eggs, beaten
freshly ground black pepper

TO GARNISH:
2 tablespoons chopped fresh parsley

1 Heat the oil in the frying pan, and fry the pepper until soft but not brown.
2 Add the ham and tuna, pour in the eggs and add the seasoning.
3 Cook over a low heat, stirring frequently, until the eggs are just set. Sprinkle with the chopped parsley and serve at once, with wholemeal toast.

Salami, Red Pepper and
Mozzarella Salad (page 15),
Spinach and Tuna Roulade (page 15),
Tuna Piperade

ASPARAGUS TURKEY ROLLS

Serves 4

300 g (10 oz) packet of frozen chopped spinach, thawed
600 ml (1 pint) semi-skimmed milk
100 g (4 oz) mushrooms, chopped very finely
40 g (1½ oz) plain flour
1 teaspoon lemon juice
salt and ground white pepper
340 g (11½ oz) can of asparagus spears, drained
100 g pack of Plumrose Turkey Slice
2 tablespoons grated Parmesan cheese

1 Preheat the oven to Gas Mark 4/180°C/350°F.
2 Dry the spinach off in a pan over a gentle heat until the moisture has evaporated. Spoon into a shallow ovenproof dish.
3 Place half the milk with the mushrooms in a pan and simmer gently for 5 minutes.
4 Blend the flour with the rest of the milk until smooth, then add to the pan. Stir over the heat until the sauce thickens, allow to simmer for 1 minute, then add the lemon juice and seasoning.
5 Divide the asparagus spears evenly between the turkey slices and roll them up. Place on top of the spinach. Chop any remaining asparagus spears and add to the mushroom sauce.
6 Pour the sauce over the asparagus rolls and sprinkle with the Parmesan cheese. Bake in the oven for 25 minutes. Serve hot with new potatoes.

NUTTY RICE RING

Serves 6

2 tablespoons sunflower oil
1 onion, chopped finely
1 small red pepper, de-seeded and chopped
2 medium-size tomatoes, skinned, de-seeded and chopped
¼ teaspoon ground turmeric
225 g (7½ oz) long-grain rice
850 ml (1¼ pint) chicken stock
255 g carton of Plumrose Savoury Roll, Garlic Sausage variety, chopped
170 g can of Plumrose Chopped Ham with Pork, chopped
50 g (2 oz) flaked almonds
salt and freshly ground black pepper

TO GARNISH:
frisée lettuce
cucumber slices

1 Heat the oil in a large frying pan and sauté the onion and pepper until soft but not brown.
2 Add the tomatoes, turmeric and rice to the pan. Stir-fry for 1 minute, then pour in the stock. Bring to the boil, cover and simmer for 20 minutes.
3 Stir the garlic sausage and chopped ham with pork into the rice mixture and cook for a further 5 minutes or until the rice is cooked and has absorbed the stock.
4 Stir in the flaked almonds and seasoning and set aside.
5 Grease a 1.1-litre (2-pint) ring mould with oil and spoon in the rice mixture, packing it down tightly in the mould. Allow to cool, then cover the mould with clingfilm and chill.
6 Turn out on to to a serving plate and serve garnished with frisée lettuce and cucumber.

Asparagus Turkey Rolls,
Nutty Rice Ring

SALAMI AND POTATO SALAD

Serves 4

DRESSING:
2 tablespoons white wine vinegar
4 tablespoons low-calorie lemon mayonnaise
2 tablespoons chopped fresh dill
salt and freshly ground black pepper

SALAD:
450 g (1 lb) tiny new potatoes, scrubbed
100 g pack of Plumrose Danish Salami, cut into strips
8 cherry tomatoes, halved
8 hard-boiled quails' eggs, halved
1 tablespoon snipped fresh chives

1 To make the dressing, stir the vinegar into the mayonnaise until blended, then add the dill and seasoning.

2 Steam the potatoes until just tender, then toss them in the dressing while still hot. Top with the salami, tomatoes and quails' eggs. Sprinkle the chives over the top.

Serve warm, or allow the potatoes to go cold before adding the salami, tomatoes, eggs and chives.

BRIE AND HAM STUFFED MUSHROOMS

Serves 4

8 large cup mushrooms
4 tablespoons olive or sunflower oil
75 g (3 oz) blue Brie cheese
1 garlic clove, crushed
56 g (½ pack, 2 slices) Plumrose Honey Ham, chopped
50 g (2 oz) fresh wholemeal breadcrumbs
freshly ground black pepper

Freezing: possible

1 Preheat the oven to Gas Mark 6/200°C/400°F.
2 Wipe the mushrooms and remove the stalks. Brush the caps with 3 tablespoons of the oil and place in an ovenproof dish in a single layer.
3 Chop the mushroom stalks finely and sauté in the remaining oil for 1 minute. Remove from the heat.
4 Cut the Brie cheese into small chunks and add to the pan with the garlic, ham and breadcrumbs. Spoon the filling into the mushrooms and grind a little black pepper over the top.
5 Bake in the oven for about 15 minutes until bubbling. Serve hot with a tomato and onion salad.

Salami and Potato Salad,
Brie and Ham Stuffed Mushrooms

MELON, PRAWN AND ORANGE SALAD

Serves 4

1 frisée lettuce
225 g (7½ oz) cottage cheese with chives
170 g (6 oz) peeled prawns
or
185 g can of Plumrose Tuna Chunks in Brine, drained and flaked
2 large oranges, peeled
1 small Ogen or Canteloupe melon
1 box mustard and cress

1 Trim the frisée lettuce and divide into small sprigs. Arrange on a serving plate or place in a glass salad bowl.
2 Mix together the cottage cheese and prawns or tuna.
3 Divide the oranges into segments. Cut the melon into chunks or small balls. Arrange the oranges and melon over the lettuce, then pile the cottage cheese and prawns mixture on top. Sprinkle with the mustard and cress. Serve at once.

SARDINE AND OLIVE PÂTÉ

Serves 2
as a light meal, 4 as a starter

125 g can of Plumrose Sardines in Oil, drained
125 g can of Plumrose Sardines in Tomato
4 tablespoons natural 8% fat fromage frais
1 teaspoon Worcestershire sauce
2 teaspoons lemon juice
4 pimento-stuffed olives, chopped
salt and ground white pepper

Freezing: possible

1 Remove and discard any bones from the sardines.
2 Place the drained sardines, sardines in tomato sauce, fromage frais, Worcestershire sauce, lemon juice and olives in a bowl and mash together. Add the seasoning.
3 Spoon the mixture into a small serving dish, cover with clingfilm and chill. Serve with slices of hot wholemeal toast.

Melon, Prawn and Orange Salad,
Sardine and Olive Pâté

PASTEL SALAD

Serves 4

100 g (4 oz) cracked wheat
1/2 iceberg lettuce, shredded
1 Sweetie grapefruit, peeled
1 green-skinned eating apple, chopped
1 small green pepper, de-seeded and chopped
1 celery stick, sliced
1 kiwi fruit, sliced
200 g (7 oz) peeled prawns
or
185 g can of Plumrose Tuna Chunks in Brine, drained
and flaked

DRESSING:
6 tablespoons walnut oil
1 tablespoon lemon juice
1 tablespoon chopped fresh tarragon
salt and freshly ground black pepper

1 Soak the cracked wheat in hot water for 30 minutes, then drain. Press in a sieve to extract the moisture.

2 Place the lettuce in a large salad bowl.

3 Divide the Sweetie grapefruit into segments, place in another bowl and add the cracked wheat, apple, green pepper, celery, kiwi fruit and prawns or tuna. Toss well.

4 To make the dressing, whisk all the ingredients together or shake well in a screw-top jar. Pour over the cracked wheat mixture and toss well.

5 Spoon into the salad bowl on top of the lettuce and toss together just before serving. Serve with crusty wholemeal bread.

MEDITERRANEAN SALAD

Serves 4

170 g (6 oz) green beans
170 g (6 oz) broad beans
170 g can of Plumrose Chopped Ham with Pork
3 tomatoes
1 head of radicchio
2 hard-boiled eggs
8 black olives

DRESSING:
6 tablespoons olive oil
2 tablespoons red wine vinegar
1 garlic clove, crushed
1 teaspoon chopped fresh thyme
salt and freshly ground black pepper

1 Trim the green beans and cut into 5 cm (2 inch) lengths. Cook the green beans and broad beans separately in boiling salted water until just tender. Drain and rinse in cold water.

2 Cut the chopped ham with pork into thin strips. Cut the tomatoes into wedges. Shred the radicchio and place in a salad bowl. Top with the green beans, broad beans, chopped ham and pork and tomatoes.

3 Cut each egg into 8 wedges. Arrange over the salad with the olives.

4 To make the dressing, whisk the ingredients together or shake well in a screw-top jar. Spoon over the salad and toss gently before serving.

Pastel Salad,
Mediterranean Salad

GARLIC SAUSAGE AND BEAN CASSOULET

Serves 4

2 tablespoons sunflower oil
8 spring onions, trimmed
1 courgette, sliced
1 red pepper, de-seeded and chopped
1 dessert apple, chopped
255 g carton of Plumrose Savoury Roll,
Garlic Sausage variety, diced
255 g carton of Plumrose Savoury Roll, Beef Roll with
Peppers variety, diced
2 tablespoons tomato purée
300 ml (½ pint) tomato juice
1 teaspoon dried sage
410 g (13½ oz) can of flageolet beans, drained
213 g (7 oz) can of butter beans, drained
salt and ground white pepper
100 g (4 oz) fresh breadcrumbs
100 g (4 oz) Cheddar cheese, grated
50 g (2 oz) block margarine

Freezing: possible

1 Heat the oil in a large pan and cook the spring onions, courgette, pepper, and apple for 5 minutes, stirring frequently.
2 Stir in the garlic sausage, beef roll with peppers, tomato purée, tomato juice, sage, flageolet beans, butter beans and seasoning. Bring to the boil, cover and simmer for 10 minutes.
3 Preheat the grill.
4 Transfer the mixture to a heatproof dish. Mix together the breadcrumbs and cheese and sprinkle a thick layer over the top. Dot with the margarine and place under the grill until browned.

STIR-FRIED CHICKEN LIVERS WITH PEPPERS

Serves 4

2 tablespoons crunchy peanut butter
2 tablespoons soy sauce
1 tablespoon white wine vinegar
1 teaspoon chilli sauce
4 tablespoons sunflower oil
225 g (7½ oz) chicken livers
170 g can of Plumrose Bacon Grill
225 g (7½ oz) Chinese leaves, shredded
100 g (4 oz) mangetout peas
1 red pepper, de-seeded and cut into strips
4 spring onions, sliced

1 Mix together the peanut butter, soy sauce, vinegar, chilli sauce and 2 tablespoons of the oil. Stir in the chicken livers until coated, then leave to marinate for four hours.
2 Cut the bacon grill into 1 cm (½ inch) chunks. Heat the remaining oil in a large frying pan or wok and stir-fry the bacon grill for 5 minutes. Remove to a plate.
3 Add the Chinese leaves, mangetout peas, red pepper and spring onions to the pan and cook for 5 minutes, tossing frequently. Remove to a plate.
4 Add the chicken livers and marinade to the pan. Stir-fry for 3–4 minutes.
5 Return the bacon grill and vegetables to the pan and toss over the heat for 2 minutes. Serve at once.

Garlic Sausage and Bean Cassoulet,
Stir-Fried Chicken Livers with Peppers

PORK AND CHIVE TORTILLA

Serves 4

2 tablespoons sunflower oil
50 g (2 oz) button mushrooms, quartered
100 g pack of Plumrose Pork Luncheon Meat
50 g (2 oz) frozen peas, defrosted
6 eggs
salt and freshly ground black pepper
1 tablespoon snipped fresh chives

1 Heat the oil in a large frying pan and cook the mushrooms until soft.
2 Cut the pork luncheon meat into 2.5 cm (1 inch) lengths. Stir into the pan, add the peas and cook for one minute.
3 Preheat the grill to high.
4 Beat together the eggs and seasoning, stir in the chives and pour into the pan. Cook over a gentle heat, drawing the mixture from the sides of the pan to the centre with a fork as it starts to set.
5 When the base of the tortilla is cooked, place the pan under the grill for 2–3 minutes to set the top. Serve at once with a mixed salad.

SALAMI AND CHICKEN PILAF

Serves 4

2 chicken breasts
600 ml (1 pint) chicken stock
225 g (7½ oz) long grain rice
1 teaspoon dried marjoram
100 g (4 oz) frozen peas, defrosted
1 red pepper, de-seeded and chopped
1 green pepper, de-seeded and chopped
100 g pack of Plumrose Danish Salami, chopped
50 g (2 oz) pine nuts
freshly ground black pepper

1 Skin and bone the chicken breasts, place in a frying pan and pour over the stock. Bring to the boil, cover and simmer for 20 minutes or until the chicken is cooked.
2 Remove the chicken breasts from the pan and cut the meat into small chunks.
3 Strain the stock into a measuring jug and make up to 600 ml (1 pint) with water. Pour back into the frying pan. Add the rice and marjoram, bring to the boil and simmer for 8 minutes.
4 Stir in the peas and peppers, bring back to simmering point and cook for 5 minutes or until all the liquid has been absorbed.
5 Stir in the salami, pine nuts, chicken and seasoning. Heat, stirring occasionally for 2–3 minutes, until piping hot. Serve with a mixed salad.

Pork and Chive Tortilla,
Salami and Chicken Pilaf

TUNA AND MUSHROOM SOUFFLÉ

Serves 3-4

198 g can of Plumrose Tuna Steaks in Oil, drained
50 g (2 oz) block margarine
50 g (2 oz) mushrooms, wiped and chopped finely
50 g (2 oz) plain flour
300 ml (½ pint) semi-skimmed milk
1 tablespoon tomato purée
salt and ground white pepper
4 egg yolks
5 egg whites

1 Preheat the oven to Gas Mark 5/190°C/375°F.
2 Brush a 1.4 litre (2½ pint) soufflé dish with oil. Flake the tuna.
3 Melt the margarine in a pan and cook the mushrooms for 3–4 minutes, stirring frequently.
4 Remove from the heat, stir in the flour, then cook for one minute. Blend in the milk and bring to the boil, stirring. Simmer for 1 minute, then stir in the tuna, tomato purée and seasoning.
5 Remove from the heat and beat in the egg yolks one at a time. Whisk the egg whites until stiff, stir 2 tablespoons into the mixture then fold in the rest.
6 Spoon into the soufflé dish and bake in the oven for 25–30 minutes until well risen, firm on top but still creamy inside. Serve at once with a green salad.

HAM AND RED PEPPER SPAGHETTI

Serves 4

350 g (12 oz) wholewheat spaghetti
3 tablespoons sunflower oil
225 g (7½ oz) button mushrooms, sliced
1 courgette, cut into matchsticks
1 red pepper, de-seeded and sliced
255 g carton of Plumrose Lean-n-Tasty Ham, cut into strips
3 eggs
170 g (6 oz) natural 8% fat fromage frais
salt and freshly ground black pepper

1 Cook the spaghetti according to the instructions on the packet. Drain.
2 Heat the oil in a large frying pan and stir-fry the mushrooms, courgette, and pepper for 5 minutes until soft but not brown. Stir in the ham.
3 In a bowl beat together the eggs, fromage frais and seasoning.
4 Add the spaghetti to the ham mixture and toss well. Pour in the egg mixture and toss over the heat until the eggs set. Serve at once.

Tuna and Mushroom Soufflé,
Ham and Red Pepper Spaghetti

BACON GRILL AND CHICKEN BURGERS

Serves 6

300 g can of Plumrose Bacon Grill, minced
1 boneless chicken breast, skinned and minced
100 g (4 oz) mushrooms, chopped finely
1 small onion, chopped finely
100 g (4 oz) fresh wholemeal breadcrumbs
1 tablespoon chopped fresh parsley
salt and freshly ground black pepper
1 (size 3) egg, beaten
flour for dusting
sunflower oil for frying

TO SERVE:
6 sesame seed wholemeal burger buns
4 lettuce leaves
1 red-skinned onion, sliced
1 tomato, sliced
pickled gherkins, sliced

Freezing: possible (uncooked)

1 In a large bowl mix together the bacon grill, chicken breast, mushrooms, onion, breadcrumbs, parsley and seasoning.
2 Add the beaten egg and stir well to bind the mixture together.
3 Divide into 6 and with floured hands shape into 6 burgers. Place on a baking sheet and chill for 30 minutes.
4 Dust with flour and shallow fry for 3–4 minutes on each side until golden. Drain on absorbent paper. Serve in burger buns with lettuce, onion rings, tomato slices and gherkin slices.

GARLIC SAUSAGE CASSEROLE

Serves 6

3 tablespoons sunflower oil
2 leeks, sliced thinly
2 garlic cloves, crushed
2 × 397 g (13 oz) cans of tomatoes
600 ml (1 pint) chicken stock
255 g carton of Plumrose Savoury Roll,
Garlic Sausage variety
255 g carton of Plumrose Lean 'n' Tasty,
Turkey Roll
415 g (13$^{1}/_{2}$ oz) can of blackeye or flageolet beans,
drained
213 g (7 oz) can of butter beans, drained
1 tablespoon black treacle
salt and freshly ground black pepper

Freezing: possible

1 Heat the oil in a large pan and sauté the leeks and garlic until soft but not brown.
2 Add the tomatoes and break them up with a wooden spoon. Pour in the stock and bring to the boil. Lower the heat and simmer for 10 minutes.
3 Cut the garlic sausage and turkey roll into large chunks. Add to the pan with the blackeye or flageolet beans and butter beans. Stir in the black treacle and seasoning.
4 Allow to simmer for 20 minutes, stirring occasionally. Serve hot with chunks of Granary bread.

*Bacon Grill and Chicken Burgers,
Garlic Sausage Casserole*

PRAWN JAMBALAYA

Serves 4

2 tablespoons sunflower oil
170 g can of Plumrose Bacon Grill, cut into strips
1 onion, chopped
1 green pepper, de-seeded and chopped
1 garlic clove, crushed
225 g (7½ oz) long-grain brown rice
397 g (13 oz) can of chopped tomatoes
600 ml (1 pint) chicken stock
250 g (8 oz) peeled prawns
113 g pack of Plumrose Honey Ham, cut into strips
salt and freshly ground black pepper
1 tablespoon chopped fresh thyme

Freezing: possible

1 Heat the oil in a large frying pan and cook the bacon grill for 5 minutes. Remove from the pan and set aside.

2 Add the onion, pepper and garlic to the pan and sauté until soft but not brown.

3 Stir in the rice, then add the tomatoes and stock. Bring to the boil, then lower the heat and cover the pan. Cook gently for about 35 minutes until the rice is almost tender and has absorbed most of the stock.

4 Stir in the prawns, ham and the reserved bacon grill. Add the seasoning and thyme. Cook for a further 10 minutes until heated through. Serve hot with a green salad.

SPAGHETTI, HAM AND PORK BAKE

Serves 4

225 g (7½ oz) spaghetti
225 g (7½ oz) broccoli
2 tablespoons sunflower oil
1 leek, sliced
1 red pepper, de-seeded and chopped
1 garlic clove, crushed
300 g can of Plumrose Chopped Ham with Pork, chopped
2 tablespoons chopped fresh parsley
salt and freshly ground black pepper
150 ml (¼ pint) fresh soured cream
100 g (4 oz) Gruyère cheese, grated

1 Preheat the oven to Gas Mark 4/180°C/350°F.

2 Cook the spaghetti according to the instructions on the packet. Drain.

3 Meanwhile, divide the broccoli into small florets and chop any long stalks. Cook in boiling salted water for 5 minutes, then drain.

4 Heat the oil and sauté the leek, pepper and garlic until soft but not brown. Remove from the heat and stir in the broccoli, chopped ham with pork, parsley and seasoning.

5 Mix together the spaghetti and ham with pork mixture then stir in the soured cream.

6 Spoon into an ovenproof dish and sprinkle with the grated cheese. Bake in the oven for 35–40 minutes, until hot and bubbling. Serve hot with a green salad.

Prawn Jambalaya,
Spaghetti, Ham and Pork Bake

SEAFOOD TAGLIATELLE

Serves 4

350 g (12 oz) mixed green and white tagliatelle
2 tablespoons olive oil
½ fennel head, sliced thinly
2 rashers back bacon, de-rinded and chopped
99 g can of Plumrose Tuna Steaks in Oil, drained
200 g (7 oz) peeled prawns
50 g (2 oz) frozen peas, defrosted
170 g (6 oz) 8% fat fromage frais
1 teaspoon cornflour
2 tablespoons Pernod or dry white wine
salt and freshly ground black pepper

TO GARNISH:
chopped fresh fennel leaves

1 Cook the tagliatelle according to the instructions on the packet. Drain.
2 Meanwhile, heat the oil in a deep frying pan and cook the fennel and bacon until the fennel is soft and the bacon lightly browned.
3 Break up the tuna with a fork and stir into the pan with the prawns, peas and pasta. Toss together over the heat for 1 minute.
4 Blend together the fromage frais, cornflour and Pernod or wine until smooth and stir into the pan. Add the seasoning and simmer for 5 minutes over a gentle heat, stirring frequently to prevent sticking. Serve hot, sprinkled with the chopped fresh fennel leaves.

VEGETABLE THATCH

Serves 4

2 tablespoons sunflower oil
1 onion, chopped
100 g (4 oz) button mushrooms, quartered
300 g can of Plumrose Pork Luncheon Meat
198 g (7 oz) can of sweetcorn with peppers, drained
425 g (14 oz) can of chopped tomatoes
1 tablespoon soy sauce
450 g (1 lb) carrots, sliced
450 g (1 lb) swede, chopped
50 g (2 oz) low-fat spread
salt and freshly ground black pepper

Freezing: possible

1 Preheat the oven to Gas Mark 4/180°C/350°F.
2 Heat the oil in a frying pan and cook the onion until soft but not brown.
3 Stir in the mushrooms and cook for 1 minute. Cut the pork luncheon meat into 1 cm (½ inch) chunks and add to the pan with the sweetcorn with peppers, tomatoes and soy sauce.
4 Bring to the boil and simmer for 15 minutes or until the liquid from the tomatoes has evaporated.
5 Cook the carrots and swede separately in boiling water until tender, drain and mash each with 25 g (1 oz) of low-fat spread, salt and pepper.
6 Spoon the luncheon meat mixture into an ovenproof dish, place alternate lines of carrots and swede over the top and rough up with a fork. Cook in the oven for about 40 minutes until hot.

Seafood Tagliatelle,
Vegetable Thatch

CHICKEN, SAUSAGE AND WATERCRESS CASSEROLE

Serves 4

3 tablespoons sunflower oil
4 chicken breasts, boned and skinned
1 leek, sliced thinly
1 bunch of watercress
100 g pack of Plumrose French-Style Garlic Sausage,
cut into thin strips
2 tablespoons cornflour
300 ml ($1/2$ pint) chicken stock
150 g (5 oz) natural yogurt
salt and freshly ground black pepper

TO GARNISH:
watercress sprigs

Freezing: possible

---

1 Heat the oil in a large frying pan and fry the chicken breasts until lightly browned on both sides. Remove and keep warm.
2 Add the leek to the pan and sauté for about 5 minutes until soft but not brown.
3 Chop the watercress finely, discarding the tough stalks, and add to the pan with the garlic sausage and chicken.
4 Blend together 1 tablespoon of the cornflour and the stock and pour into the pan. Bring to the boil, stirring, then lower the heat, cover and simmer gently for 30 minutes until the chicken is cooked.
5 Stir the remaining cornflour into the yogurt and stir into the pan. Bring back to the boil and simmer for 1 minute. Garnish with watercress sprigs and serve with new potatoes.

SWEET AND SOUR CHICKEN AND FRANKFURTERS

Serves 4

227 g ($7^1/2$ oz) can of pineapple slices in natural juice
100 g (4 oz) cranberries
1 tablespoon soft brown sugar
1 tablespoon soy sauce
4 spring onions
2 tablespoons sunflower oil
1 green pepper, de-seeded and sliced
2 chicken breasts
2.5 cm (1 inch) piece of root ginger, peeled and
chopped finely
can of 6 Plumrose Hot Dog Sausages
1 teaspoon cornflour
150 ml ($1/4$ pint) chicken stock
salt and freshly ground black pepper

Freezing: possible

---

1 Drain the pineapple slices and place the juice in a saucepan with the cranberries, sugar and soy sauce. Simmer for about 5 minutes until the cranberries are tender. Set aside.
2 Cut the pineapple into small chunks and set aside.
3 Cut the spring onions into 2.5 cm (1 inch) lengths. Heat the oil in a large frying pan or wok and stir-fry the pepper and spring onions for 3 minutes.
4 Skin and slice the chicken breasts into thin strips, add to the pan with the ginger and stir-fry for 5 minutes.
5 Cut the hot dog sausages into 1 cm ($1/2$ inch) lengths and add to the pan with the pineapple chunks. Stir-fry for 1 minute, then pour in the cranberry mixture.
6 Blend the cornflour with the stock and stir into the pan. Add the seasoning. Bring to the boil, stirring, then simmer for one minute until thickened. Serve with boiled rice.

Also pictured on the front cover

*Chicken, Sausage and Watercress Casserole,
Sweet and Sour Chicken and Frankfurters*

MACARONI GRATIN

Serves 6

100 g (4 oz) wholewheat macaroni
300 g (10 oz) packet of frozen spinach, thawed
2 tablespoons sunflower oil
1 onion, chopped
1 yellow pepper, de-seeded and chopped
225 g (7½ oz) cooked carrots, sliced
185 g can of Plumrose Tuna Chunks in Brine, drained
and flaked
200 g (7 oz) peeled prawns
295 g (10 oz) can of condensed asparagus soup
salt and freshly ground black pepper
275 g (9 oz) natural yogurt
2 (size 3) eggs, beaten
1 large tomato, sliced thinly
50 g (2 oz) Cheddar cheese, grated

Freezing: possible

1 Preheat the oven to Gas Mark 4/180°C/350°F.
2 Cook the macaroni according to the instructions on the packet then drain.
3 Place the spinach in a pan and dry off over a gentle heat until all the moisture has evaporated.
4 Meanwhile, heat the oil in a frying pan and fry the onion and pepper until soft but not brown. Remove from the heat and stir in carrots, tuna, prawns, macaroni and the soup until evenly blended. Add the seasoning.
5 Transfer the spinach to a shallow ovenproof dish and spread out over the base. Spoon the macaroni mixture on top.
6 Beat together the yogurt and eggs and pour over the macaroni mixture.
7 Top with halved tomato slices and the grated Cheddar cheese. Bake in the oven for 45 minutes. Serve with a green salad.

Macaroni Gratin,
Crusty Bread Pizzas (page 42),
Sausage and Lentil Pot (page 42)

CRUSTY BREAD PIZZAS

Serves 4

1 small wholemeal French stick
4 tablespoons passata or other tomato pasta sauce

TOPPING:
1 small onion, preferably red-skinned
½ green pepper
113 g pack of Plumrose Apple Ham, chopped
1 pineapple ring, chopped
100 g (4 oz) mozzarella cheese, sliced

1 Preheat the grill to high.
2 Cut the French stick in half lengthways and divide each half in two. Toast the cut sides until lightly browned.
3 Slice the onion into fine rings. Cut the green pepper into thin strips.
4 Spread the toasted bread with the pasta sauce and top with the chopped ham, onion rings, pineapple, pepper and slices of cheese.
5 Place under the grill until the cheese melts. Serve hot.

Pictured on page 41

SAUSAGE AND LENTIL POT

Serves 4

2 tablespoons sunflower oil
2 onions, sliced
1 garlic clove, crushed
2 × 397 g (13 oz) cans of tomatoes
100 g (4 oz) split red lentils
150 ml (¼ pint) chicken stock
150 ml (¼ pint) dry cider
1 teaspoon dried oregano
can of 30 Plumrose Party Sausages
salt and freshly ground black pepper

1 Heat the oil in a large flameproof casserole or saucepan and cook the onions and garlic until soft but not brown.
2 Add the tomatoes, lentils, stock, cider, oregano and sausages and bring to the boil.
3 Cover and simmer gently for about 50 minutes (stirring occasionally to break up the tomatoes) until the lentils are tender. Add the seasoning. Serve with baked potatoes.

Pictured on page 41

PORK AND AVOCADO BASKETS

Serves 6
12 thin slices of wholemeal bread 5 tablespoons sunflower oil FILLING: 198 g can of Plumrose Pork Luncheon Meat, chopped ½ small avocado, chopped 2 teaspoons lemon juice 2.5 cm (1 inch) piece of cucumber, diced finely 78 g (2½ oz) packet of garlic and herb cream cheese

1 Preheat the oven to Gas Mark 5/190°C/375°F.
2 Using a fluted cutter, stamp out twelve 7.5 cm (3 inch) rounds from the bread slices. Roll the bread rounds with a rolling pin until very thin.
3 Brush on both sides with the oil and press into tartlet tins.
4 Bake in the oven for 15 minutes until brown and crisp.
5 Divide the pork luncheon meat between the bread cases. Toss the avocado and lemon juice together and divide between the cases with the cucumber.
6 Spoon a little garlic cream cheese on top of each tartlet and return them to the oven for about 10 minutes, until the cheese melts. Serve hot with a potato salad.

Pictured on page 45

TUNA AND PRAWN GRATIN

Serves 4
2 tablespoons oil 1 leek, sliced 1 green pepper, de-seeded and chopped ¼ cucumber, diced finely 1 tablespoon chopped fresh dill 400 ml (¾ pint) fish or chicken stock 50 g (2 oz) cornflour 150 ml (¼ pint) unsweetened orange juice 1 tablespoon tomato purée 100 g (4 oz) button mushrooms, sliced ½ teaspoon Worcestershire sauce 185 g can of Plumrose Tuna Chunks in Brine, drained and rinsed 200 g (7 oz) peeled prawns salt and ground white pepper 700 g (1½ lb) potatoes, mashed 1 tablespoon sesame seeds *Freezing: possible*

1 Heat the oil in a frying pan and cook the leek and green pepper until soft but not brown.
2 Stir in the cucumber and dill and cook for 1 minute.
3 Stir a little of the stock into the cornflour until smooth. Add to the pan with the remaining stock and orange juice.
4 Bring to the boil, stirring until the sauce is thick and smooth, and cook for 1 minute. Add the tomato purée, mushrooms and Worcestershire sauce.
5 Lower the heat and simmer gently for 10 minutes. Stir in the tuna, prawns and seasoning and heat for a further 5 minutes.
6 Preheat the grill.
7 While the tuna mixture is cooking spoon the mashed potato into a piping bag fitted with a large star nozzle and pipe around the edge of a shallow ovenproof dish.
8 Spoon the tuna mixture into the middle of the piped potato shell. Sprinkle with the sesame seeds and place under the grill until the potatoes are lightly browned.

Pictured on page 45

SPINACH-STUFFED POTATOES

Serves 4

4 large even-sized potatoes,
weighing about 275 g (9 oz) each
1 garlic clove, crushed
100 g (4 oz) cooked chopped spinach, well drained
56 g (½ pack, 2 slices) Plumrose Smokey Ham, chopped
100 g (4 oz) Gruyère cheese, grated
salt, freshly ground black pepper
and a pinch of ground nutmeg
½ red pepper, de-seeded and sliced

1 Preheat the oven to Gas Mark 6/200°C/400°F.

2 Scrub the potatoes and prick all over with a fork. Place on a baking sheet and bake in the oven for 1–1¼ hours until soft when pressed.

3 Cut the tops off the potatoes, scoop out the flesh into a bowl, and mash.

4 Stir in the garlic, spinach, ham and 50 g (2 oz) of the cheese. Add the seasoning.

5 Spoon the filling back into the potato skins, packing it down tightly. Top each one with a pepper slice and a little of the remaining cheese.

6 Return to the oven for 10–15 minutes to heat through and melt the cheese.

Note:

The potatoes can also be cooked by microwave. Scrub and prick them with a fork. Arrange in a circle on a sheet of absorbent paper. Microwave at 100% (high) for about 20 minutes until soft. Return the filled potatoes to the microwave for 1–2 minutes until the cheese melts.

Pork and Avocado Baskets (page 43),
Tuna and Prawn Gratin (page 43),
Spinach-Stuffed Potatoes

MUSHROOM AND GARLIC SAUSAGE RISOTTO

Serves 4

2 tablespoons sunflower oil
6 spring onions, sliced
1 carrot, sliced thinly
2 courgettes, sliced
1 garlic clove, crushed
100 g (4 oz) mushrooms, sliced
225 g (7½ oz) long-grain brown rice
900 ml (1½ pints) chicken stock
255 g carton of Plumrose Savoury Roll,
Garlic Sausage variety
170 g can of Plumrose Chopped Ham with Pork
170 g (6 oz) beansprouts
salt and freshly ground black pepper

1 Heat the oil in a large pan and fry the spring onions and carrot for about 5 minutes.
2 Stir in the courgettes, garlic and mushrooms and cook for a further 2 minutes.
3 Stir in the rice, add the stock and bring to the boil. Cover and simmer for 35 minutes.
4 Cut the garlic sausage and chopped ham with pork into 1 cm (½ inch) chunks and add to the pan with the bean sprouts. Cover and simmer for a further 10 minutes until the rice is cooked and has absorbed all the stock. Add the seasoning.

FOUR CHEESE AND SAUSAGE PIZZA

Serves 4

225 g (7½ oz) wholemeal flour
2 teaspoons baking powder
50 g (2 oz) block margarine
150 ml (¼ pint) semi-skimmed milk
1 tablespoon French mustard
2 tablespoons sunflower oil
1 onion, sliced
50 g (2 oz) mushrooms, sliced
397 g (13 oz) can of chopped tomatoes
100 g pack of Plumrose French-Style Garlic Sausage,
chopped
40 g (1½ oz) each of Red Leicester, Lancashire, Sage
Derby and Cotswold cheeses, grated

Freezing: possible

1 Place the flour in a bowl and mix in the baking powder. Rub in the margarine, then stir in enough of the milk to mix to a soft dough.
2 Knead on a lightly floured surface until smooth, then roll out to a 23 cm (9 inch) square. Lift onto a baking sheet and spread with the mustard.
3 Preheat the oven to Gas Mark 6/200°C/400°F.
4 Heat the oil in a frying pan and cook the onion until soft but not brown. Add the mushrooms and cook for a further 1 minute.
5 Add the tomatoes, bring to the boil and allow to bubble until most of the excess moisture has evaporated.
6 Remove from the heat and allow to cool a little. Spoon over the pizza base and top with the garlic sausage.
7 Cover with the cheeses, placing a different cheese over each quarter of the pizza. Bake in the oven for 25-30 minutes until the cheese is golden and bubbling. Serve hot with a salad.

Mushroom and Garlic Sausage Risotto,
Four Cheese and Sausage Pizza

HAM, BEAN AND CAULIFLOWER SALAD

Serves 4

DRESSING:
3 tablespoons olive oil
1 tablespoon white wine vinegar
1 tablespoon light soy sauce
1 tablespoon sesame seeds
salt and freshly ground black pepper

SALAD:
100 g (4 oz) green beans
1 cauliflower
1 bunch of watercress
170 g can of Plumrose Chopped Ham with Pork, cut into strips
50 g (2 oz) pine nuts

1 Whisk the dressing ingredients together in a bowl or shake in a screw-top jar until blended.
2 Cut the green beans into 5 cm (2 inch) lengths. Divide the cauliflower into small florets. Cook together in boiling salted water until just tender. Drain. Toss them in the dressing while still hot. Allow to cool.
3 Divide the watercress into small sprigs and add to the salad with the chopped ham with pork and pine nuts. Toss well before serving.

TUNA-FILLED CROISSANTS

Serves 4

4 croissants
low-fat spread
4 lettuce leaves, shredded finely
185 g can of Plumrose Tuna Chunks in Brine, drained
1 tablespoon tomato ketchup
2 tablespoons natural yogurt
1 hard-boiled egg, chopped
salt and freshly ground black pepper
1 box mustard and cress

1 Split the croissants in half horizontally and spread with low-fat spread.
2 Divide the shredded lettuce evenly between the croissants.
3 Flake the tuna into a bowl and mix in the ketchup, yogurt, hard-boiled egg and seasoning.
4 Spoon the tuna mixture over the lettuce, dividing it evenly between the croissants. Top with mustard and cress.
5 Replace the croissant tops and wrap in clingfilm until needed.

Ham, Bean and Cauliflower Salad,
Tuna-Filled Croissants

FRUIT AND NUT COLESLAW

Serves 8-10

½ white cabbage
¼ red cabbage
198 g can of Plumrose Pork Luncheon Meat
50 g (2 oz) raisins
2 tablespoons sunflower seeds
50 g (2 oz) pecan nuts

DRESSING:
1 garlic clove, crushed
8 tablespoons sunflower oil
3 tablespoons cider vinegar
½ teaspoon dried oregano
a pinch of celery salt
4 tablespoons low-calorie mayonnaise
salt and ground white pepper

1 Cut away any hard centre core from the white and red cabbage. Shred the leaves very finely and place in a large bowl.
2 Cut the pork luncheon meat into thin sticks and add to the bowl with the raisins, sunflower seeds and pecans. Toss well.
3 To make the dressing, place the garlic in a small pan with the oil, cider vinegar, oregano and celery salt. Bring to the boil, whisking all the time, then remove from the heat and whisk in the mayonnaise. Add the seasoning. Pour over the cabbage mixture and toss to coat, then leave to cool. Store in a covered plastic container until needed.

TRIPLE DECKERS

Serves 4

4 Granary or wholemeal baps
low-fat spread
50 g (½ pack, 4 slices) of Plumrose German-Style Liver Sausage
75 g (3 oz) cooked beetroot, chopped
2 tablespoons fresh soured cream
1 teaspoon chopped fresh dill
1 tablespoon cranberry sauce
50 g (½ pack, 2½ slices) of Plumrose Chicken Slice
watercress sprigs

1 Cut each bap horizontally into 3 slices. Stand the four base slices on a board and spread with a little low-fat spread. Top each one with a slice of liver sausage.
2 Mix together the beetroot, soured cream and chopped dill and spread over the liver sausage.
3 Spread the centre slices with a little cranberry sauce, then place them over the beetroot mixture. Top with slices of chicken and a few watercress sprigs. Replace the tops of the baps. Wrap in clingfilm until needed.

Fruit and Nut Coleslaw,
Triple Deckers,
Waldorf Turkey Salad with Tuna Dressing (page 52),
Turkey and Feta Cheese Pittas (page 52)

WALDORF TURKEY SALAD WITH TUNA DRESSING

Serves 4

1/2 iceberg lettuce, shredded
1 eating apple, chopped
1 tablespoon lemon juice
2 celery sticks, sliced
50 g (2 oz) chopped walnuts
50 g (2 oz) raisins
255 g carton of Plumrose Savoury Roll,
Turkey variety, chopped

DRESSING:
99 g can of Plumrose Tuna Steaks in Oil
3 tablespoons natural yogurt
3 tablespoons low-calorie mayonnaise
1 teaspoon lemon juice
salt and a pinch of paprika

1 Place the lettuce in a bowl. Toss the apple in the lemon juice and add to the bowl with the celery, walnuts, raisins and turkey roll. Toss until well combined.
2 To make the dressing, liquidise or mash together the tuna and its oil, yogurt, mayonnaise and lemon juice. Add the seasoning.
3 To serve, spoon the dressing over the salad.

Pictured on page 51

TURKEY AND FETA CHEESE PITTAS

Serves 4

4 pitta breads
1 tablespoon horseradish sauce
170 g (6 oz) feta cheese
100 g pack of Plumrose Turkey Slice
5 cm (2 inch) piece of cucumber, diced
1/2 yellow pepper, de-seeded and chopped
2 small tomatoes, chopped

1 Slit each pitta bread open down the side. Spread the inside of each pocket with a little horseradish sauce.
2 Cut the feta cheese into small chunks and place in a bowl. Cut each slice of turkey into quarters and add to the bowl with the cucumber, pepper and tomatoes.
3 Spoon the mixture into the pitta breads, dividing it equally. Serve at once.
Note:
For a packed lunch, cut the pockets in the pitta bread at home but pack the filling in a separate plastic box. Fill the pittas when you are ready to eat. Don't forget to pack a spoon for this.

Pictured on page 51

CHEESY HAM MUFFINS

Serves 4

4 wholemeal muffins
low-fat spread
4 tablespoons tomato or sweetcorn relish
170 g can of Plumrose Chopped Ham with Pork, chopped
100 g (4 oz) mozzarella cheese, sliced
4 small pickled gherkins, chopped

1 Preheat the grill.
2 Split the muffins in half and toast lightly on both sides.
3 Spread the cut sides with a little low-fat spread and the relish.
4 Top each muffin half with chopped ham with pork, mozzarella cheese and chopped gherkin. Grill until the cheese melts and bubbles. Serve immediately.

Pictured on page 55

POTATO AND HAM SCRAMBLE

Serves 4

700 g (1½ lb) small new potatoes
4 tablespoons sunflower oil
1 onion, sliced
1 green pepper, de-seeded and chopped
1 celery stick, chopped
25 g (1 oz) block margarine
6 (size 3) eggs, beaten
2 tablespoons skimmed milk
salt and freshly ground black pepper
170 g can of Plumrose Chopped Ham with Pork, chopped
1 tablespoon snipped fresh chives

1 Scrub the potatoes and cut into 5 mm (¼ inch) slices without peeling. Cook in boiling salted water for 3–4 minutes, or until just tender. Drain.
2 Heat the oil in a frying pan and add the potatoes. Fry for about 10 minutes until the potato slices are starting to brown, turning them occasionally. Add the onion, pepper and celery and fry for a further 5 minutes.
3 Transfer the potato mixture to a serving dish and keep warm.
4 Melt the margarine in a saucepan and add the beaten eggs, milk and seasoning. Stir over a medium heat until the eggs start to set.
5 Stir in the chopped ham with pork and continue to cook until the eggs are just set. Spoon into the centre of the potato mixture, sprinkle with the chives and serve at once.

Pictured on page 55

TUNA AND BEAN SALAD

Serves 4

415 g (13½ oz) can of red kidney beans, drained and rinsed
275 g (9 oz) can of butter beans, drained and rinsed
170 g (6 oz) cooked broad beans
¼ cucumber, cut into matchsticks
2 carrots, grated
198 g can of Plumrose Tuna Steaks in Oil

DRESSING:
drained oil from tuna can
2 tablespoons tomato purée
2 tablespoons lemon juice
1 tablespoon sesame seeds
salt and freshly ground black pepper

1 Place the kidney beans, butter beans, broad beans, cucumber and carrots in a bowl.
2 Drain the tuna, reserving the oil in another bowl. Flake the fish and add to the vegetables. Toss until combined.
3 To make the dressing, whisk the tomato purée and lemon juice into the tuna oil. Stir in the sesame seeds and seasoning.
4 Pour the dressing over the salad and toss well before serving.

Cheesy Ham Muffins (page 53),
Potato and Ham Scramble (page 53),
Tuna and Bean Salad

MACKEREL PASTIES

Makes 10

PASTRY:
225 g (7½ oz) plain flour
100 g (4 oz) block margarine
½ teaspoon dry mustard
1 (size 3) egg yolk
about 1 tablespoon cold water

FILLING:
125 g can of Plumrose Mackerel Fillets in Tomato
2 tablespoons sunflower oil
6 spring onions, chopped
100 g (4 oz) button mushrooms, chopped
1 tablespoon lemon juice
75 g (3 oz) ricotta cheese
salt and freshly ground black pepper
beaten egg to glaze

Freezing: possible

1 To make the pastry, sift the flour into a bowl and rub in the margarine until the mixture resembles fine breadcrumbs.
2 Stir in the mustard, egg yolk and enough water to bind together. Knead lightly on a floured board, then wrap in clingfilm and chill for 1 hour.
3 Preheat the oven to Gas Mark 6/200°C/400°F.
4 To make the filling, flake the mackerel into a bowl, discarding any bones. Mash with the tomato sauce.
5 Heat the oil in a pan and fry the onions and mushrooms until soft but not brown. Allow to cool then stir into the mackerel with the lemon juice. Beat in the ricotta cheese and the seasoning.
6 Roll out the pastry 5 mm (¼ inch) thick on a lightly floured surface and cut into 10 even-sized squares, re-rolling the trimmings.
7 Spoon a little filling onto the first square of pastry and brush the edges with water. Fold one corner over the filling to meet the opposite corner and press the edges together to make a triangular pasty. Repeat with the remaining squares, dividing the filling evenly between them.
8 Lift the pasties onto baking sheets, cover with clingfilm and chill for 30 minutes.
9 Brush the pasties with beaten egg and bake in the oven for 20 minutes, until golden brown.

Mackerel Pasties,
Harlequin Loaf (page 58),
Ham and Courgette Tarts (page 58)

HARLEQUIN LOAF

Serves 6

1 small Granary or wholemeal loaf
low-fat spread

CHICKEN FILLING:
100 g pack of Plumrose Chicken Slice, chopped
50 g (2 oz) sultanas
1 celery stick, chopped
3 tablespoons low-calorie mayonnaise
1 teaspoon curry paste

EGG FILLING:
25 g (1 oz) butter
2 (size 3) eggs, beaten
2 tablespoons milk
50 g (½ pack, 4 slices) Plumrose French-Style Garlic Sausage, chopped
salt and ground white pepper

AVOCADO FILLING:
1 avocado
1 teaspoon lemon juice
a dash of Tabasco sauce

---

1 Cut the loaf horizontally into four layers and spread the cut surfaces with a little low-fat spread.
2 To make the chicken filling, mix all the ingredients together in a bowl until evenly combined. Set aside.
3 To make the egg filling, melt the butter in a saucepan and add the eggs and milk. Cook over a gentle heat, stirring constantly, until the eggs are set. Remove from the heat and stir in the garlic sausage and seasoning. Set aside.
4 To make the avocado filling, mash together the avocado, lemon juice and Tabasco sauce. Set aside.
5 Spread each of the three bottom layers of the loaf with a different filling, reassemble the loaf and replace the top. Wrap in foil and chill. Serve cut into vertical slices.

Pictured on page 57

HAM AND COURGETTE TARTS

Makes 12

PASTRY:
275 g (9 oz) plain flour
75 g (3 oz) rolled oats
170 g (6 oz) block margarine
a little cold water

FILLING:
2 tablespoons sunflower oil
6 spring onions, sliced thinly
1 small courgette, sliced thinly
113 g pack of Plumrose Honey Ham, chopped
300 ml (½ pint) semi-skimmed milk
3 eggs
salt and pepper

Freezing: possible

---

1 To make the pastry, sift the flour into a bowl, add the oats and rub in the margarine. Add enough water to mix to a soft dough.
2 Knead lightly on a floured surface until smooth, then wrap in clingfilm and chill for 30 minutes.
3 Preheat the oven to Gas Mark 6/200°C/400°F.
4 To make the filling, heat the oil in a frying pan and fry the onions and courgette over a low heat until softened. Set aside.
5 Roll out the pastry on a lightly floured surface and line twelve 10 cm (4 inch) Yorkshire pudding tins, using a cutter or small saucer as a template.
6 Divide the onion and courgette mixture and the ham evenly between the pastry cases.
7 Beat together the milk, eggs and seasoning. Pour into the pastry cases. Bake in the oven for 25–30 minutes or until the filling is set and starting to brown. Serve hot or cold with a potato salad.

Pictured on page 57

BACON GRILL AND MUSHROOM PIES

Makes 8

PASTRY:
300 g (10 oz) plain flour
50 g (2 oz) block margarine
50 g (2 oz) white vegetable fat
50 g (2 oz) ground almonds
a little cold water

FILLING:
1 tablespoon sunflower oil
50 g (2 oz) mushrooms, chopped
170 g can of Plumrose Bacon Grill, chopped
75 g (3 oz) Lancashire cheese, grated
1 tablespoon chopped fresh thyme
2 tablespoons creamed horseradish
salt and pepper
beaten egg to glaze

Freezing: possible

1 To make the pastry, sift the flour into a bowl and rub in the margarine and vegetable fat. Stir in the ground almonds, then add enough water to mix to a soft dough.
2 Knead lightly on a floured surface until smooth, then wrap in clingfilm and chill for 1 hour.
3 Preheat the oven to Gas Mark 6/200°C/400°F.
4 To make the filling, heat the oil in a frying pan and cook the mushrooms and bacon grill for 5 minutes, stirring occasionally. Transfer to a bowl and allow to cool.
5 Stir in the cheese, thyme, creamed horseradish and seasoning.
6 Roll out just over half the pastry on a lightly floured surface and cut out eight 11.5 cm (4½ inch) rounds. Place on a baking sheet.
7 Divide the filling equally between the pastry rounds and brush the edges with water.
8 Roll out the remaining pastry and cut out eight 10 cm (4 inch) rounds. Lift the lids over the filling, pressing the pastry edges together to seal. Cut a small hole in the top of each. Brush with beaten egg and bake in the oven for 25–30 minutes until golden brown. Serve hot or cold.

Pictured on page 61

HERBY SAUSAGE SWIZZLES

Serves 6

170 g (6 oz) plain flour
75 g (3 oz) block margarine
1 teaspoon dried thyme
a little cold water
beaten egg to glaze
can of 6 Plumrose Hot Dog Sausages,
drained and rinsed

FOR DIPPING:
low-sugar tomato ketchup or mild mustard

Freezing: possible

1 Sift the flour into a bowl and rub in the margarine until the mixture resembles fine breadcrumbs. Stir in the dried thyme.
2 Add enough water to mix to a firm dough. Knead lightly on a floured surface until smooth then wrap in clingfilm and chill for 1 hour.
3 Preheat the oven to Gas Mark 6/200°C/400°F.
4 Roll out the pastry on a lightly floured surface and cut into 1 cm (½ inch) strips.
5 Brush the strips with beaten egg and wrap around the hot dog sausages in an overlapping spiral, enclosing them completely.
6 Place on a baking sheet and brush with beaten egg. Bake in the oven for 10–15 minutes until golden brown. Serve with a small pot of low-sugar tomato ketchup or mild mustard for dipping.

Pictured on page 61

CURRIED PASTA SPIRAL SALAD

Serves 4

100 g (4 oz) mangetout peas
170 g (6 oz) three-colour pasta spirals
1 avocado, peeled and chopped
1 tablespoon lemon juice
225 g can of Plumrose Party Sausages, halved
100 g pack of Plumrose Bavarian Style Ham Sausage
8 cherry tomatoes, halved
1 celery stick, sliced

DRESSING:
150 g (5 oz) natural yogurt
6 tablespoons low-calorie mayonnaise
1 teaspoon curry paste

1 Top and tail the mangetout peas and cook in boiling water for 2 minutes. Drain in a colander and cool under cold running water.
2 Cook the pasta spirals as directed on the packet. Drain and rinse with hot water. Submerge in a bowl of cold water to cool.
3 Toss the avocado in the lemon juice and place in a large bowl. Add the mangetout peas, drained pasta spirals, sausages, ham sausage, tomatoes and celery and mix well.
4 To make the dressing, beat together the yogurt, mayonnaise and curry paste. Spoon the mixture over the salad and toss well.

Bacon Grill and Mushroom Pies (page 59),
Herby Sausage Swizzles (page 59),
Curried Pasta Spiral Salad

HAM AND TURKEY PIE

Serves 6

PASTRY:
170 g (6 oz) wholemeal flour
170 g (6 oz) plain flour, sifted
a pinch of salt
100 g (4 oz) white vegetable fat
150 ml (1/4 pint) water

FILLING:
1 eating apple, chopped
1 teaspoon lemon juice
160 g (1/2 carton) of Plumrose Slicing Joint, Turkey variety, chopped
320 g carton of Plumrose Slicing Joint, Ham variety, chopped
2 teaspoons chopped fresh sage
freshly ground black pepper
2 hard-boiled eggs
beaten egg to glaze
2 teaspoons gelatine
300 ml (1/2 pint) chicken stock

1 Preheat the oven to Gas Mark 6/200°C/400°F.

2 To make the pastry, place the flours and salt in a bowl. Heat together the vegetable fat and water until the fat melts, then add to the flours and stir to make a soft dough.

3 Knead until smooth, then roll out two thirds on a lightly floured surface and use to line the base and sides of a 900 g (2 lb) loaf tin. Set aside the remaining pastry.

4 To make the filling, in a bowl mix together the apple, lemon juice, turkey, ham and sage. Add the seasoning.

5 Spoon half the meat mixture into the pastry-lined tin and top with the whole hard-boiled eggs, pressing them down lightly. Cover the eggs with the remaining meat mixture.

6 Roll out the remaining pastry. Brush the edge of the pastry case with water and cover the filling with the remaining rolled out pastry. Trim the edges and press together to seal.

7 Decorate the top with any pastry trimmings cut into leaves, fixing these in place by brushing them with water.

8 Make a small hole in the top of the pie, then glaze with beaten egg. Bake in the oven for 30 minutes, then reduce the temperature to Gas Mark 4/180°C/350°F and bake for a further 30 minutes until the pastry is golden brown. Allow the pie to cool in the tin.

9 Dissolve the gelatine in the stock and cool a little before carefully pouring it into the pie through the hole in the top. Chill to allow the jelly to set before removing the pie from the tin. Serve cut into thick slices with salad.

Ham and Turkey Pie,
Wholemeal Scone Roulade (page 64),
Pork and Vegetable Samosas (page 64)

WHOLEMEAL SCONE ROULADE

Serves 4

FILLING:
2 tablespoons sunflower oil
1 celery stick, chopped
50 g (2 oz) button mushrooms, sliced
1 small courgette, chopped
113 g pack of Plumrose Smokey Ham, cut into strips

ROULADE:
275 g (9 oz) wholemeal self-raising flour
a pinch of salt
1/4 teaspoon dry mustard
50 g (2 oz) block margarine
50 g (2 oz) Edam cheese, grated
150 ml (1/4 pint) semi-skimmed milk
beaten egg to glaze

Freezing: possible

1 To make the filling, heat the oil and sauté the celery until just soft. Add the mushrooms and courgette and cook for a further 1 minute.
2 Remove from the heat and stir in the ham. Allow to cool.
3 Preheat the oven to Gas Mark 7/220°C/425°F.
4 To make the roulade, mix the flour, salt and mustard together in a bowl, then rub in the margarine. Stir in the cheese, then mix in enough milk to make a soft dough.
5 Knead lightly on a floured surface until smooth, then roll out to a 25.5 × 20.5 cm (10 × 8 inch) rectangle.
6 Spoon the filling over the dough and roll up from one long side. Lift onto a greased baking sheet and brush with beaten egg.
7 Bake in the oven for 30 minutes or until golden brown. Serve hot or cold cut into thick slices.

Pictured on page 63

PORK AND VEGETABLE SAMOSAS

Makes 10

225 g (7½ oz) potatoes
½ small cauliflower
2 tablespoons sunflower oil
4 spring onions, chopped
2 teaspoons ground coriander
1 teaspoon ground cumin
198 g can of Plumrose Pork Luncheon Meat, chopped
2 tomatoes, peeled, de-seeded and chopped
10 sheets of filo pastry
sunflower oil for brushing
4 tablespoons mango chutney, chopped
2 tablespoons sesame seeds

Freezing: possible

1 Cut the potatoes into small chunks and divide the cauliflower into small florets. Cook separately in boiling salted water until just tender. Drain and set aside.
2 Preheat the oven to Gas Mark 5/190°C/375°F.
3 Heat the oil in a frying pan and fry the onions until soft but not brown. Stir in the spices and cook for 1 minute.
4 Stir in the potatoes, cauliflower, pork luncheon meat and tomatoes until evenly coated in the onions and spices. Remove from the heat and allow to cool.
5 Lay one sheet of filo pastry on the work surface (keep remainder covered with a damp cloth) and brush with oil.
6 Spread a little mango chutney in the centre and add some of the pork luncheon meat mixture.
7 Fold the pastry over the filling on each side and roll up in a log shape. Repeat with the remaining pastry sheets, dividing the chutney and filling evenly between them. Place on a greased baking sheet and brush with oil. Sprinkle with sesame seeds. Bake in the oven for about 20 minutes, until golden brown and crisp. Serve hot.

Pictured on page 63 and on the back cover

CHICKEN AND ASPARAGUS CHEESECAKE

Serves 12

PASTRY:
350 g (12 oz) plain flour
170 g (6 oz) block margarine
a little cold water

FILLING:
340 g (11¹/2 oz) can of asparagus spears, drained
100 g pack of Plumrose Chicken Slice, chopped
50 g (2 oz) block margarine
50 g (2 oz) cornflour
150 ml (¹/4 pint) chicken stock
300 ml (¹/2 pint) semi-skimmed milk
1 teaspoon French mustard
170 g (6 oz) mature Cheddar cheese, grated
100 g (4 oz) Red Leicester cheese, grated
3 (size 3) eggs, separated
1 tablespoon snipped fresh chives

Freezing: possible

1 To make the pastry, sift the flour into a bowl and rub in the margarine. Mix in enough water to make a soft dough.

2 Knead lightly on a floured surface until smooth, then roll out to line a 23 cm (9 inch) spring clip tin. Chill for 1 hour.

3 Preheat the oven to Gas Mark 6/200°C/400°F.

4 Line the pastry case with greaseproof paper and fill with baking beans. Bake in the oven for 15 minutes, remove the beans and paper and bake for a further 5 minutes. Remove the pastry from the oven, then reduce the temperature to Gas Mark 4/180°C/350°F.

5 To make the filling, arrange the asparagus spears in the bottom of the pastry case. Scatter the chopped chicken slice over the top.

6 Melt the margarine in a saucepan and stir in the cornflour. Cook for 1 minute then remove from the heat and stir in the stock and milk. Bring to the boil, stirring, then add the mustard and cheeses. Stir until the cheese melts, then remove from the heat.

7 Beat in the egg yolks and add the chives. Whisk the egg whites until stiff and fold into the mixture.

8 Pour into the pastry case and bake for 1¹/4 to 1¹/2 hours until set and golden brown. Allow to cool, then chill. Serve cut in wedges.

Pictured on page 67

CHILLI BEAN AND HAM SOUP

Serves 6

3 tablespoons sunflower oil
1 onion, chopped
3 celery sticks, chopped
1 garlic clove, crushed
425 g (14 oz) can of chopped tomatoes with herbs
300 ml (½ pint) chicken stock
300 ml (½ pint) tomato juice
a few drops of Tabasco sauce
170 g can of Plumrose Chopped Ham with Pork
425 g (14 oz) can of red kidney beans, drained
salt and ground paprika

Freezing: possible

1 Heat the oil in a large saucepan and fry the onion, celery and garlic until soft but not brown.
2 Add the chopped tomatoes, chicken stock, tomato juice and Tabasco sauce and bring to the boil.
3 Cut the chopped ham with pork into matchsticks and stir into the pan with the kidney beans. Cover and simmer for 20 minutes. Add the seasoning.
Note:
For a packed lunch, spoon the mixture into a wide-necked Thermos flask. Wholemeal herb and garlic bread, wrapped in foil to keep it hot, makes a good accompaniment.

TURKEY TURNOVERS

Serves 6

225 g (7½ oz) wholemeal pastry
(see Ham and Chicory Tartlets recipe, page 9)
2 tablespoons cranberry sauce
100 g (4 oz) cooked carrots, chopped
100 g (4 oz) cooked green beans, chopped
50 g (2 oz) cooked mushrooms, chopped
100 g pack of Plumrose Turkey Slice, chopped
1 tablespoon chopped fresh parsley
salt and freshly ground black pepper
beaten egg to glaze

Freezing: possible

1 Preheat the oven to Gas Mark 6/200°C/400°F.
2 Roll out the pastry on a lightly floured surface and cut out 6 rounds using a 15 or 18 cm (6 or 7 inch) teaplate as a guide. Spread the pastry rounds with the cranberry sauce.
3 Mix together the carrots, beans, mushrooms, turkey slice, parsley and seasoning.
4 Divide the filling between the pastry rounds and brush the pastry edges with beaten egg.
5 Fold the pastry rounds in half to enclose the filling and press the edges together to seal. Lift onto a baking sheet.
6 Brush the turnovers with beaten egg and bake in the oven for 20 minutes, until brown. Serve hot or cold with salad.

*Chicken and Asparagus Cheesecake (page 65),
Chilli Bean and Ham Soup,
Turkey Turnovers*

HAM AND EGG PARCELS

Makes 12

PASTRY:
170 g (6 oz) self-raising flour, sifted
170 g (6 oz) wholemeal flour
75 g (3 oz) block margarine
75 g (3 oz) white vegetable fat
a little hot water

FILLING:
255 g carton of Plumrose Savoury Roll, Ham and
Chicken variety, chopped
1 hard-boiled egg, chopped
100 g (4 oz) ricotta or curd cheese
1 tablespoon low-sugar tomato ketchup
beaten egg to glaze

1 Preheat the oven to Gas Mark 6/200°C/400°F.
2 To make the pastry, place the flours in a bowl and rub in the margarine and vegetable fat. Add enough cold water to make a soft dough. Knead until smooth then roll out on a lightly floured surface and cut into 12 × 9 cm (5 × 3½ inch) squares.
3 To make the filling, mix together the ham and chicken roll and egg, then stir in the cheese and ketchup.
4 Brush the edges of each pastry square with water and spoon a little filling into the centre. Fold the corners to the centre over the filling and press the edges together to seal.
5 Lift the parcels onto a baking sheet and brush with beaten egg. Bake in the oven for 25 minutes or until golden.

STAR FISH CAKES

Serves 4

375 g (12 oz) cod fillets, cooked and skinned
185 g can of Plumrose Tuna Chunks in Brine, drained
450 g (1 lb) boiled potatoes, mashed
1 (size 3) egg, beaten
1 tablespoon snipped fresh chives
salt and ground white pepper

COATING:
50 g (2 oz) plain flour
2 (size 3) eggs, beaten
75 g (3 oz) dry breadcrumbs
oil for shallow frying

Freezing: possible

1 Flake the cod and tuna into a bowl. Stir in the mashed potato then add enough beaten egg to bind the mixture together, reserving any leftover egg for the coating. Add the chives and seasoning. Cover and chill for 1 hour.
2 Divide the mixture into 8 and shape into flat star-shaped cakes or small fish shapes. Coat with flour, dip into the beaten egg, then coat with the breadcrumbs.
3 Shallow fry in hot oil for about 7 minutes until golden brown, turning once. Drain on absorbent paper. Serve hot with peas or baked beans.

Ham and Egg Parcels,
Star Fishcakes

CREAMY PASTA SHELLS WITH MINI BURGERS

Serves 4

225 g (7½ oz) pasta shells, plain or wholewheat
2 tablespoons sunflower oil
2 celery sticks, sliced
1 green pepper, de-seeded and chopped
368 g can of Plummies Mini Burgers in BBQ Sauce
2 large tomatoes, peeled, de-seeded and chopped
295 g (10 oz) can of condensed cream of mushroom soup
50 g (2 oz) Cheddar cheese, grated
freshly ground black pepper

1 Cook the pasta shells according to the instructions on the packet. Drain.
2 Heat the oil in a large saucepan and cook the celery and pepper until soft.
3 Add the mini burgers, and the tomatoes, stir well then add the drained pasta shells and pour in the soup. Bring slowly to the boil, stirring frequently. Simmer for 2 minutes. Add the cheese and the seasoning and stir over the heat until the cheese melts. Serve hot.

SAUSAGE CROQUETTES

Serves 6

450 g (1 lb) potatoes, boiled
2 teaspoons low-fat spread
56 g (½ pack, 2 slices) Plumrose Apple Ham, chopped
50 g (2 oz) Wensleydale cheese, grated
freshly ground black pepper
can of 6 Plumrose Hot Dog Sausages, drained and rinsed
3 tablespoons plain flour
1 (size 3) egg, beaten
100 g (4 oz) dry wholemeal breadcrumbs
sunflower oil for shallow frying

Freezing: possible

1 Mash the potatoes with the low-fat spread. Stir in the ham, cheese and pepper.
2 Divide the potato mixture into 6 and mould each portion around a hot dog sausage. Coat with flour, brush with beaten egg, then roll in the breadcrumbs.
3 Heat about 1 cm (½ inch) oil in a large frying pan and fry the croquettes for about 10 minutes until golden brown on all sides. Drain on absorbent paper. Serve hot with grilled tomatoes.

SAVOURY RICE WITH MEATBALLS

Serves 4

2 tablespoons oil
100 g (4 oz) mushrooms, sliced
170 g (6 oz) long grain rice
400 ml (¾ pint) chicken stock
100 g (4 oz) frozen peas
368 g can of Plummies Meatballs in Rich Gravy or Mini Burgers in BBQ Sauce
salt and ground white pepper

1 Heat the oil in a large frying pan and fry the mushrooms for 3 minutes.
2 Stir in the rice, then add the stock. Bring slowly to the boil, cover and cook over a gentle heat for 30 minutes, stirring occasionally.
3 Stir in the frozen peas, meatballs or mini burgers and seasoning. Re-cover the pan and cook for a further 10 minutes until the rice is tender and has absorbed all the stock. Serve hot.

Creamy Pasta Shells with Mini Burgers,
Sausage Croquettes,
Savoury Rice with Meatballs

PARTY SANDWICHES

125 g can of Plumrose Sardines in Oil, drained
3 tablespoons low-calorie mayonnaise
12 thin slices of wholemeal bread
low-fat spread

Freezing: possible

1 Remove the bones from the sardines and mash with the mayonnaise until smooth.
2 Spread the slices of bread with a little low-fat spread.
3 Spread six slices with a little of the filling and sandwich with the remaining slices of bread.
4 Cut out small figures or shapes using fancy animal biscuit cutters or gingerbread men cutters.
5 Keep sandwiches wrapped in clingfilm until ready to serve.

VARIATIONS:

125 g can of Plumrose Mackerel Fillets in Brine, drained
50 g (2 oz) cottage cheese
Mash the mackerel with the cottage cheese until smooth. Fill sandwiches as above.

6 tablespoons cheese spread
198 g can of Plumrose Pork Luncheon Meat, sliced thinly
Spread slices of bread with a little cheese spread and top with slices of luncheon meat. Finish as above.

EGG IN A NEST

Serves 4

450 g (1 lb) potatoes
225 g (7½ oz) carrots, sliced
4 tablespoons sunflower oil
113 g pack of Plumrose Honey Ham
100 g (4 oz) Gouda cheese, diced finely
4 (size 3) eggs

1 Cut the potatoes into large chunks and boil with the carrots for 5 minutes. Drain. Cut the potatoes into small even-sized pieces.
2 Preheat the oven to Gas Mark 4/180°C/350°F.
3 Heat the oil in a frying pan and fry the potatoes and carrots for about 15 minutes until the potatoes are golden, stirring occasionally.
4 Chop the ham into small chunks and add to the pan with the cheese.
5 Spoon the mixture into 4 small ovenproof dishes. Make a well in the centre of each and break an egg into it. Bake in the oven for 15 minutes or until the eggs are set.

Party Sandwiches,
Egg in a Nest

PORK AND MINI BURGER HOT POT

Serves 4-6

900 g (2 lb) potatoes, sliced thinly
3 tablespoons sunflower oil
1 large onion, sliced
1 green pepper, de-seeded and chopped
100 g pack of Plumrose Pork Luncheon Meat, chopped
368 g can of Plummies Mini Burgers in Rich Gravy
salt and freshly ground black pepper
50 g (2 oz) Edam cheese, grated

Freezing: possible

1 Cook the potatoes in boiling salted water for 5 minutes or until just tender. Drain.
2 Preheat the oven to Gas Mark 5/190°C/375°F.
3 Heat the oil in a frying pan and fry the onion and pepper until soft but not brown. Remove from the pan.
4 Fry the potato slices in batches until lightly browned, adding a little more oil if necessary.
5 Cut the luncheon meat into 2.5 cm (1 inch) lengths and mix together with the mini burgers, onion and pepper and the seasoning.
6 Spoon into an ovenproof dish, cover with the potato slices and sprinkle with the cheese. Bake in the oven for 30 minutes until hot and bubbling. Serve hot.

BACON GRILL BUNS

Serves 4

4 wholemeal hamburger buns
4 tablespoons tomato relish
170 g can of Plumrose Bacon Grill
5 cm (2 inch) piece of cucumber, sliced
100 g (4 oz) Edam cheese, sliced

1 Preheat the grill.
2 Split the buns and lightly toast the inside. Spread each bottom half with tomato relish.
3 Cut the bacon grill into 8 slices and grill under a medium heat for 5 minutes, turning once. Drain on absorbent paper.
4 Place 2 slices of bacon grill on the bottom half of each bun and top with cucumber and cheese slices.
5 Place under the grill at a high heat for a few minutes until the cheese melts. Replace the tops of the buns and serve hot, with coleslaw or potato salad.

Pork and Mini Burger Hot Pot,
Bacon Grill Buns

PINWHEEL SANDWICHES

Makes 24

4 slices of wholemeal bread, cut from a sandwich loaf
75 g tub of Plumrose Farmhouse Spreading Pâté,
e.g. Liver and Mushroom or Brussels variety
50 g (2 oz) cottage cheese with chives
1 tablespoon low-sugar tomato ketchup

1 Cut off the crusts and flatten the bread slices with a rolling pin.
2 Beat together the spreading pâté, cottage cheese and ketchup until smooth.
3 Spread the bread slices with the mixture and roll them up from one short side like a swiss roll. Wrap the rolls tightly in cling film and twist the ends. Chill for 3–4 hours or longer.
4 To serve, unwrap and cut each roll into 6 slices.

SURPRISE SCOTCH EGGS

Makes 4

4 hard-boiled eggs, chopped
2 tablespoons low-calorie mayonnaise
170 g can of Plumrose Bacon Grill
100 g (4 oz) Cheddar cheese, grated
50 g (2 oz) plain flour
1 (size 3) egg, beaten
75 g (3 oz) wholemeal breadcrumbs
oil for deep frying

1 Mix the chopped eggs with the mayonnaise until well combined, then shape into 4 small balls on a floured surface.
2 Mince the bacon grill, or chop very finely and mix together with the cheese, flour and beaten egg.
3 Mould the bacon grill mixture around the chopped egg and mayonnaise balls, then roll them in breadcrumbs to coat.
4 Deep fry in hot oil for about 8 minutes until golden. Drain on absorbent paper and leave to cool.

BABY PIZZAS

Serves 6

BASE:
225 g (7½ oz) wholemeal self-raising flour
50 g (2 oz) block margarine
2 spring onions, chopped finely
about 150 ml (¼ pint) skimmed milk

TOPPING:
1 tablespoon olive oil
1 onion, chopped
1 garlic clove, crushed
397 g (13 oz) can of chopped tomatoes with herbs
1 tablespoon tomato purée
1 teaspoon dried oregano
a pinch of sugar
salt and freshly ground black pepper
170 g can of Plumrose Chopped Ham with Pork, chopped
50 g (2 oz) Emmenthal cheese, grated

Freezing: possible

1 To make the base, place the flour in a bowl and rub in the margarine until the mixture resembles breadcrumbs. Stir in the onions, then enough milk to make a soft dough.
2 Knead lightly on a floured surface until smooth, then wrap in clingfilm and chill for 30 minutes.
3 Preheat the oven to Gas Mark 6/200°C/400°F.
4 To make the topping, heat the oil in a pan and fry the onion and garlic until soft but not brown.
5 Add the tomatoes, tomato purée and dried oregano and simmer uncovered for about 15 minutes until reduced and thick, stirring from time to time.
6 Add the sugar and seasoning. Remove from heat.
7 Meanwhile, roll out the dough on a lightly floured surface about 5 mm (¼ inch) thick and cut into twelve 7.5 cm (3 inch) rounds using a plain cutter, re-rolling the trimmings.
8 Lift the dough onto a greased baking sheet and spread with the tomato mixture. Top with the chopped ham and a little grated cheese. Bake in the oven for about 15 minutes until the dough is risen and the cheese is bubbling.

Pinwheel Sandwiches,
Surprise Scotch Eggs, Baby Pizzas

All recipes are indexed by Plumrose product type. Some appear in more than one category.

The Plumrose Healthier Eating Cookbook Order Form

If you have enjoyed using the *Plumrose Healthier Eating Cookbook*, please tell your friends about it and let them order a copy.

The *Plumrose Healthier Eating Cookbook* is also an ideal gift.

Please send me ... copies of the *Plumrose Healthier Eating Cookbook* at £5.49* per copy (including postage & packing).

I enclose my cheque/postal order for £...... made payable to

Plumrose Ltd., Cook Book Offer,
P O Box 25, Willerby, Hull, HU10 6DR

PLEASE PRINT CLEARLY

Mrs/Ms/Miss/Mr

Address

Post Code

* Price quoted applies whilst stocks of this edition last. In the case of changes in postal or handling charges the price may be subject to review. Please allow 28 days for delivery.

The Plumrose Healthier Eating Cookbook Order Form

If you have enjoyed using the *Plumrose Healthier Eating Cookbook*, please tell your friends about it and let them order a copy.

The *Plumrose Healthier Eating Cookbook* is also an ideal gift.

Please send me ... copies of the *Plumrose Healthier Eating Cookbook* at £5.49* per copy (including postage & packing).

I enclose my cheque/postal order for £...... made payable to

Plumrose Ltd., Cook Book Offer,
P O Box 25, Willerby, Hull, HU10 6DR

PLEASE PRINT CLEARLY

Mrs/Ms/Miss/Mr

Address

Post Code

* Price quoted applies whilst stocks of this edition last. In the case of changes in postal or handling charges the price may be subject to review. Please allow 28 days for delivery.

The Plumrose Healthier Eating Cookbook Order Form

If you have enjoyed using the *Plumrose Healthier Eating Cookbook*, please tell your friends about it and let them order a copy.

The *Plumrose Healthier Eating Cookbook* is also an ideal gift.

Please send me ... copies of the *Plumrose Healthier Eating Cookbook* at £5.49* per copy (including postage & packing).

I enclose my cheque/postal order for £...... made payable to

Plumrose Ltd., Cook Book Offer,
P O Box 25, Willerby, Hull, HU10 6DR

PLEASE PRINT CLEARLY

Mrs/Ms/Miss/Mr

Address

Post Code

* Price quoted applies whilst stocks of this edition last. In the case of changes in postal or handling charges the price may be subject to review. Please allow 28 days for delivery.

The Plumrose Healthier Eating Cookbook Order Form

If you have enjoyed using the *Plumrose Healthier Eating Cookbook*, please tell your friends about it and let them order a copy.

The *Plumrose Healthier Eating Cookbook* is also an ideal gift.

Please send me ... copies of the *Plumrose Healthier Eating Cookbook* at £5.49* per copy (including postage & packing).

I enclose my cheque/postal order for £...... made payable to

Plumrose Ltd., Cook Book Offer,
P O Box 25, Willerby, Hull, HU10 6DR

PLEASE PRINT CLEARLY

Mrs/Ms/Miss/Mr

Address

Post Code

* Price quoted applies whilst stocks of this edition last. In the case of changes in postal or handling charges the price may be subject to review. Please allow 28 days for delivery.

The Plumrose Healthier Eating Cookbook Order Form

If you have enjoyed using the *Plumrose Healthier Eating Cookbook*, please tell your friends about it and let them order a copy.

The *Plumrose Healthier Eating Cookbook* is also an ideal gift.

Please send me ... copies of the *Plumrose Healthier Eating Cookbook* at £5.49* per copy (including postage & packing).

I enclose my cheque/postal order for £...... made payable to

Plumrose Ltd., Cook Book Offer,
P O Box 25, Willerby, Hull, HU10 6DR

PLEASE PRINT CLEARLY

Mrs/Ms/Miss/Mr

Address

Post Code

* Price quoted applies whilst stocks of this edition last. In the case of changes in postal or handling charges the price may be subject to review. Please allow 28 days for delivery.

The Plumrose Healthier Eating Cookbook Order Form

If you have enjoyed using the *Plumrose Healthier Eating Cookbook*, please tell your friends about it and let them order a copy.

The *Plumrose Healthier Eating Cookbook* is also an ideal gift.

Please send me ... copies of the *Plumrose Healthier Eating Cookbook* at £5.49* per copy (including postage & packing).

I enclose my cheque/postal order for £...... made payable to

Plumrose Ltd., Cook Book Offer,
P O Box 25, Willerby, Hull, HU10 6DR

PLEASE PRINT CLEARLY

Mrs/Ms/Miss/Mr

Address

Post Code

* Price quoted applies whilst stocks of this edition last. In the case of changes in postal or handling charges the price may be subject to review. Please allow 28 days for delivery.